Scary SEA MONSTERS

Gareth Stevens Publishing

Please visit our Web site www.garethstevens.com. For a free color catalog of all our high-quality books, call toll free 1-800-542-2595 or fax 1-877-542-2596.

Library of Congress Cataloging-in-Publication Data
Jackson, Tom, 1972-
Scary sea monsters / Tom Jackson.
p. cm. -- (Dangerous animals)
Includes index.
ISBN 978-1-4339-4046-0 (library binding)
ISBN 978-1-4339-4047-7 (pbk.)
ISBN 978-1-4339-4048-4 (6-pack)
1. Marine animals--Juvenile literature. 2. Sea monsters--Juvenile literature. I. Title.
QL122.2.J33 2011
591.6'509162--dc22
2010011541

Published in 2011 by
Gareth Stevens Publishing
111 East 14th Street, Suite 349
New York, NY 10003

For Gareth Stevens Publishing:
Art Direction: Haley Harasymiw
Editorial Direction: Kerri O'Donnell

For The Brown Reference Group Ltd:
Editorial Director: Lindsey Lowe
Managing Editor: Tim Harris
Editor: Tom Jackson
Children's Publisher: Anne O'Daly
Design Manager: David Poole
Designer: Supriya Sahai
Picture Manager: Sophie Mortimer
Production Director: Alastair Gourlay

Picture Credits:
Front Cover: Natural Visions: Heather Angel.

Inside: Alamy: Bill Bachman 15b; Corbis: Norbert Wu/Science Faction 15t; FLPA: Dr Bruce Robison/Minden Pictures 8, Norbert Wu/Minden Pictures 3, 9t; Hippocampus Bildarchiv: 12; iStockphoto: Ivan Choong 4, Tajammul Abidally 22, Grafissimo 20, Rainforest Australia 5t; Photolibrary: Fitor Angel 10/11, Paul Kay 28/29; Science Photo Library: Christian Darkin 16, Gregory Ochocki 5br; Shutterstock: Joe Belanger 25t, Marcus Efler 27, Stephan Kerkhofs 25b, Peter Leahy 7t. Johnny Lye 7cr, Xavier Marchant 30, Bernd Neeser 19t; Thinkstock: 18.

All Artworks The Brown Reference Group Ltd.

Printed in the United States of America
1 2 3 4 5 6 7 8 9 12 11 10

CPSIA compliance information: Batch #CS10GS: For further information contact Gareth Stevens, New York, New York at 1-800-542-2595.

CONTENTS

Any words that appear in the text in **bold** are explained in the glossary.

WHAT IS A SEA MONSTER?

The ocean is big. Even Earth's tallest mountains could disappear into its deepest parts. What lives in all that water? There are plenty of sea monsters—and they could attack at any time!

Sailors have told stories about sea monsters for hundreds of years. They talked about gigantic creatures that pulled ships underwater and fierce killers that bit holes in boats. They even said that sea serpents wrapped themselves around people and pulled them underwater, never to be seen again. Surely these are just stories? Well, sailors do like to tell tall tales: they even thought sea cows were beautiful mermaids! However, the ocean is home to some giant killers—and some small ones, too. And they are out there somewhere under all that water.

The most dangerous sea monster is also found on land. It is a monster crocodile. This creature is so at home in water that it swims across the sea from island to island. Be warned, it eats hundreds of people every year—you could be next! But it is not just the big animals that spell danger. Invisible jellyfish, tiny octopuses, and ugly looking fish can also kill you in the time it takes to read this book!

UP CLOSE

Deep-sea hunters have to search hard to find food. And they must kill anything that comes close enough for them to catch. As a result, some sea monsters have huge teeth.

Invisible Killers

The biggest killer in the ocean is impossible to see: There are more **viruses** in a glass of seawater than there are people on Earth! Most are harmless to us, but the viruses kill a fifth of all sea life each day!

BLUE-RINGED OCTOPUS

It may look cute, but this little octopus is one of the deadliest animals on Earth. One tiny nip will kill you in minutes. It is so dangerous that it is against the law to keep them as pets in some countries.

An octopus is related to snails, clams, and mussels, only they have lost their shells—and are much smarter. Blue-ringed octopuses live in the Pacific Ocean. They grip **prey** with their suckered **tentacles** and kill with a bite from their sharp beak. The **saliva** contains poison, and there is no known cure for a bite from a blue-ringed octopus.

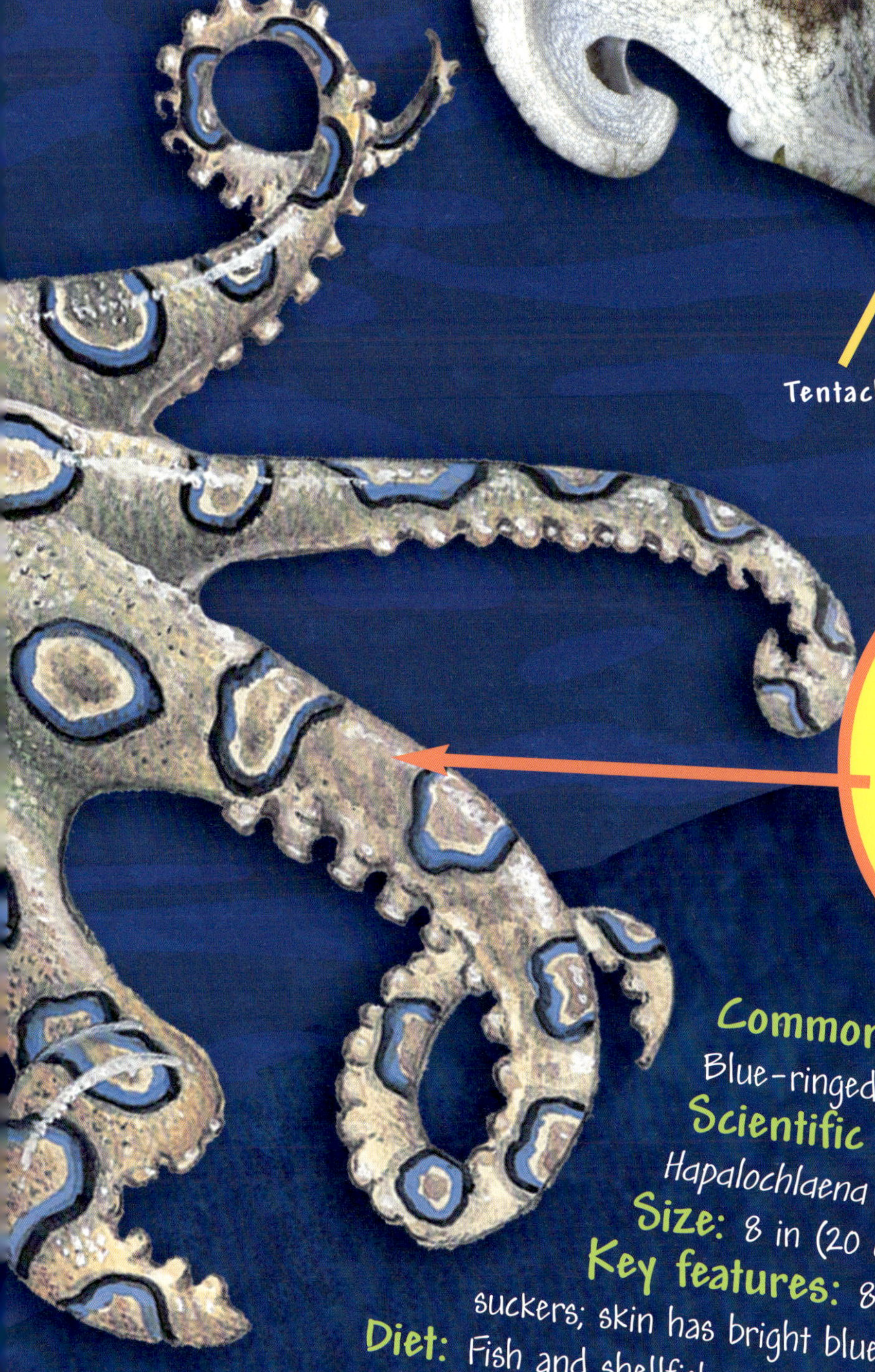

UP CLOSE

Octopuses can change the color of their skin. Their rings become bright blue as a warning that they are about to bite.

Common name: Blue-ringed octopus

Scientific name: *Hapalochlaena lunulata*

Size: 8 in (20 cm) across

Key features: 8 tentacles with suckers; skin has bright blue rings

Diet: Fish and shellfish are killed with **venom**

COMMON FANGTOOTH

The ferocious fangtooth hunts in the gloom of deep water. Few of its victims escape from its enormous teeth.

Few fish live as deep as the common fangtooth. This hunter patrols waters up to 16,400 feet (5,000 m) down. The fangtooth likes to stay out of sight in dark water. It comes near the surface on dark nights, when only starlight is shining on the water. It is difficult to find food in dark, empty water, so the fangtooth cannot afford to be fussy. Its long teeth ensure that the fangtooth will always be able to bite a big chunk out of whatever prey swims by.

UP CLOSE

The fangtooth has the largest teeth of any fish, when you compare them to the size of its whole body. When the fangtooth closes its mouth, the two longest **fangs** on the lower jaw slot into spaces on either side of the fish's brain!

Common name: Common fangtooth
Scientific name: *Anoplogaster cornuta*
Size: 6 in (15 cm)
Key features: Giant, pointed teeth; small eyes; dark body has a deep groove along both sides
Diet: Fish

GROOVY

The fangtooth cannot see much in the dark. It finds prey by sensing ripples in the water with a groove, or **lateral line**, that runs along the body.

ELECTRIC CATFISH

Prepare to be shocked! The electric catfish may look like a giant sausage with whiskers, but if you touch it you will get a strong electric shock. The shock is not enough to kill, but you won't want to touch the fish twice.

Electric catfish live only in Africa. They sit on the bottom of rivers waiting for smaller fish to swim by. The catfish lets out a series of small pulses to startle its victim. Then it moves closer to blast the victim with a full-powered shock. The prey is not killed by the electricity, but it is so stunned that it can no longer swim. The catfish then gobbles down its victim while it is still alive.

Power Lines

The catfish stores electricity in two bands of **cells, nerves,** and jelly that run from behind the head to the tail. These electric organs can produce pulses of electricity for up to 30 seconds, easily enough to stun prey.

Common name: Electric catfish
Scientific name: Malapteruridae
Size: 5 in (13 cm) to 48 in (1.2 m)
Key features: Six **barbels** (or whiskers); sausage-shaped body with **mottled** skin, small eyes; rounded fins
Diet: Small fish

UP CLOSE

Like all catfish, this type has fleshy whiskers around its mouth. The proper name for them is barbels. They are used to feel for small fish swimming nearby in the dark water.

FROGMOUTH

This river fish is not a pretty sight. Its flat head and enormous mouth make the catfish look a bit like a frog—only with spiky fins and a tail. This ugly fish lives and kills alone.

Frogmouth catfish live in the rivers of southern Asia. They are most at home buried in the thick mud on the bottom of slow-moving streams. Their fish prey are taken by surprise when a catfish attacks at great speed. The catfish slurps down victims whole with its mighty mouth.

Mouth Trap

Frogmouths wiggle the barbels on their lips so they look like tasty worms. Any fish that comes closer to take a look is snapped up!

CATFISH

Croak!

Frogmouth catfish are not named only for their wide mouths. Some of them croak when they are lifted out of the water.

UP CLOSE

A big mouth does not just help with swallowing prey. When a frogmouth needs to move fast, it gulps up water and squirts it out of the gills. That creates a surge of water that jets the fish forward.

Common name: Frogmouth catfish
Scientific name: Chacidae
Size: Around 8 in (20 cm)
Key features: Flat head with large mouth; six or eight barbels (fleshy whiskers) around mouth; tiny eyes
Diet: Fish

LARGETOOTH SAWFISH

This giant fish is related to sharks. It looks a lot like them, but there is one big difference. Sawfish do not have a mouth full of teeth—the teeth stick out of the sides of their snout instead!

The largetooth sawfish is the largest type of sawfish in the world. It grows as long as a bus! The fish lives in the Indian and Pacific Oceans and often swims up rivers to find food. The giant fish kills fish by slashing them with its saw-shaped snout.

Falling Numbers

Largetooth sawfish are very rare. Fishers catch the giant fish for their fin meat. The long saws are displayed in temples or sold as souvenirs. Catching sawfish is now banned in many countries.

Common name: Largetooth sawfish
Scientific name: *Pristis microdon*
Size: From 20 feet (6 m) to 46 feet (14 m) long
Key features: Long, narrow snout with teeth around the edge; flat body with sharklike fins
Diet: Fish

UP CLOSE

A largetooth sawfish has between 14 and 22 teeth on either side of its long snout, or saw. The biggest sawfish have saws more than 8 feet (2.4 m) long!

GULPER EEL

You might find this fact hard to swallow, but a gulper eel can swallow prey that is larger than itself! It is all thanks to a massive mouth and a tummy that can stretch like a balloon.

Gulper eels never see the sun. They live way down below the surface. The water is so deep that sunlight never gets there—even in the middle of the day. Gulper eels have very stretchy skin without many muscles underneath, so they cannot swim very well. They cannot chase prey. Instead they **lure** it toward them in the dark using a light that glows on the tip of their tail.

All Tied Up

A few gulper eels are pulled to the surface in fishing nets. Some of the eels have been found with their long, thin tail tied up in several knots.

Common name: Gulper eel
Scientific name: *Eurypharynx pelecanoides*
Size: 23 in (58 cm) to 39 in (1 m)
Key features: Huge mouth with tiny teeth; long, thin tail with light **organ**
Size: Fish and other deep-sea animals

Eye, Sea

Gulper eels have tiny eyes, but there is not much to see in the deep, dark water. The only light comes from other animals—including the eels. They make light by mixing chemicals inside a special organ.

JAPANESE

There are not many fish that are big enough to block out the sun, but if you were diving in the ocean and a devil ray swam overhead you would certainly take notice. Some are big and strong enough to tow a motorboat!

Devil rays are also called mantas, which is the Spanish word for "cloak." The rays flap their wide fins around their body, like a swirling cloak. They almost fly through the water. Devil rays look very scary, but they are only dangerous if you are a small fish or a tiny **plankton** creature.

Babies

Female devil rays give birth to their babies. It takes 13 months for a baby to grow inside its mom, and it is 3 feet (0.9 m) wide at birth.

Water Filter

Devil rays sift out tiny shrimplike creatures and other plankton from mouthfuls of water. The water is sifted by the gills as it is pumped out of long slits under the body.

DEVIL RAY

UP CLOSE

Devil rays suck in shoals of fish and swallow them whole. The rays do have hundreds of teeth in their mouths, but they are all very small.

Common name: Japanese devil ray
Scientific name: *Mobula japanica*
Size: 10 feet (3.1 m)
Key features: Body is as wide as it is long; hornlike fins stick out from head
Diet: Plankton and small fish

KILLER WH

These whales, which are also called orcas, got their name for a reason. Working alone or in packs, they hunt down almost anything in the sea. They hunt other whales and even great white sharks!

These whales were named 250 years ago by sailors who saw the great hunters attacking other whales. The sailors thought that the "killer" whales would also eat humans if they got the chance.

ALE

World Traveler

Killer whales live in more places than just about any other type of sea animal. They live in all the oceans and in all climates—from icy **polar** seas to warm **tropical** waters.

Pods

Killer whales live in families called pods. A large pod has 50 members. Just one of them is an adult male. The rest are females and their children. The whales call to each other, and each pod uses its own special sounds.

Common name: Killer whale, or orca
Scientific name: *Orcinus orca*
Size: 15 feet (4.6 m) to 29.5 feet (9 m)
Key features: Black and white body with flat tail **flukes** and rounded flippers; the males have the tallest triangular **dorsal fin** on the back
Diet: Fish, squid, seals, seabirds, and whale calves

SALTWATER

Every year "salties" eat about 1,000 people. And experts are warning that these seagoing monster crocodiles are getting to like the taste of human flesh.

Saltwater crocodiles are the world's largest reptiles. The big ones are longer than a baseball pitcher's mound, and they will attack just about anything. The crocodiles hunt along the water's edge, but they also make long journeys across the sea—and sometimes bite small boats!

UP CLOSE

Have you ever shed "crocodile tears"—pretended to cry? Crocodiles do produce tears, but not because they are sad. Instead, the tears are used to remove salt from the crocodile's body. Too much salt is bad even for killer crocs.

CROCODILE

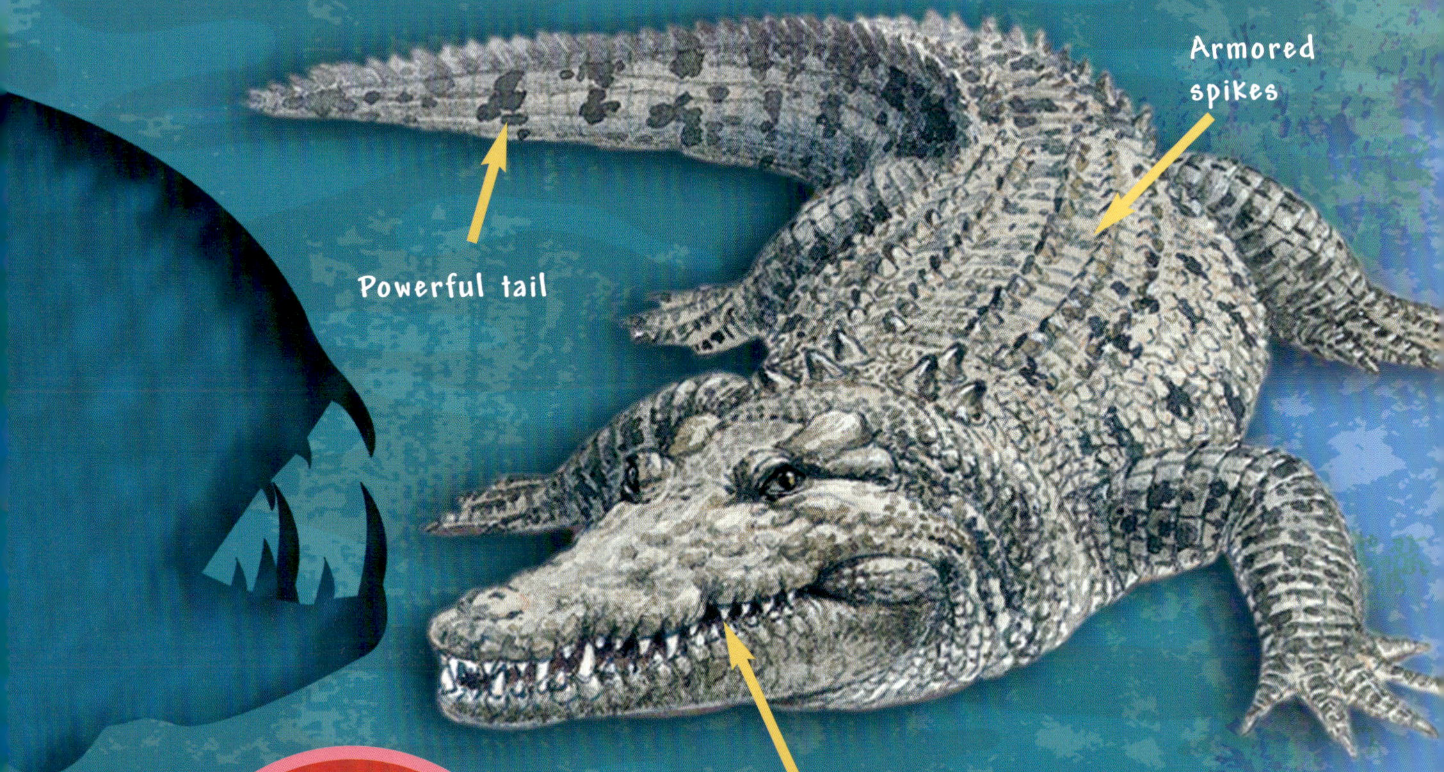

Armor

Crocodiles have thick bone under their skin. They need this armor to protect them in fights.

Common name: Saltwater crocodile
Scientific name: *Crocodylus porosus*
Size: 23 feet (7 m)
Key features: Huge jaws; four legs; powerful tail; armored with bony plates
Diet: Fish, birds, sharks, buffalo, humans

Egg Time

Crocodiles bury their eggs in an earth nest. Eggs that get warm or cold grow into females. Eggs at medium **temperatures** develop into little male crocs.

MORAY EEL

Lurking in their lairs among colorful coral reefs, moray eels are hard to spot. They only show themselves when they lunge forward to grab prey in their powerful jaws.

Moray eels are the largest and fiercest eels in the world. The giant moray eels of the Indian and Pacific Oceans grow to almost twice as long as a human. They have been known to give reef divers a dangerous bite. By the time you see a moray eel, it may be too late. During the day, they hide in long cracks in reefs with just their head poking out. An eel's body is also covered in a **camouflage** pattern, making it harder to spot as it patrols the reef at night looking for .

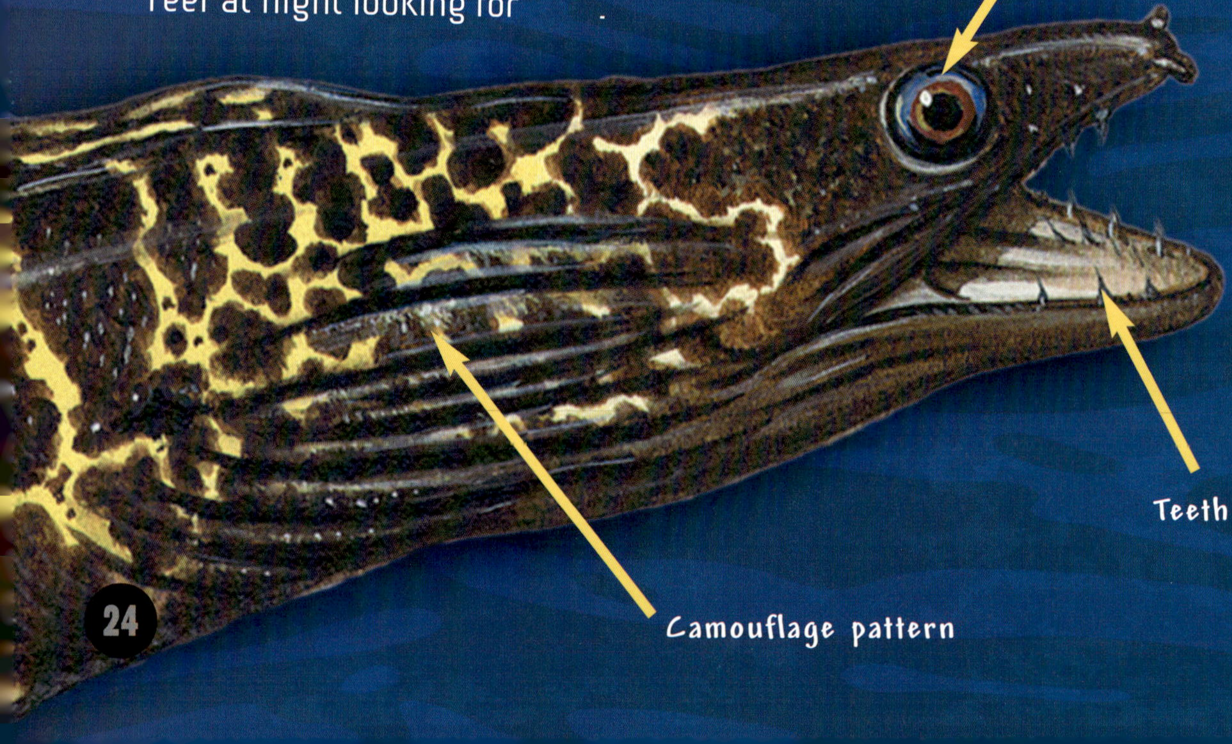

UP CLOSE

Most morays have backward-facing teeth that hook on to prey as they struggle to escape. They have a second row of teeth in their throat to help crush food as it is swallowed.

Common name: Moray eel
Scientific name: *Muraenidae*
Size: Up to 10 feet (3 m)
Key features: Pointed head with large jaws and long pointed teeth; body and tail form a paddle shape
Diet: Fish and crabs

NAUTILUS

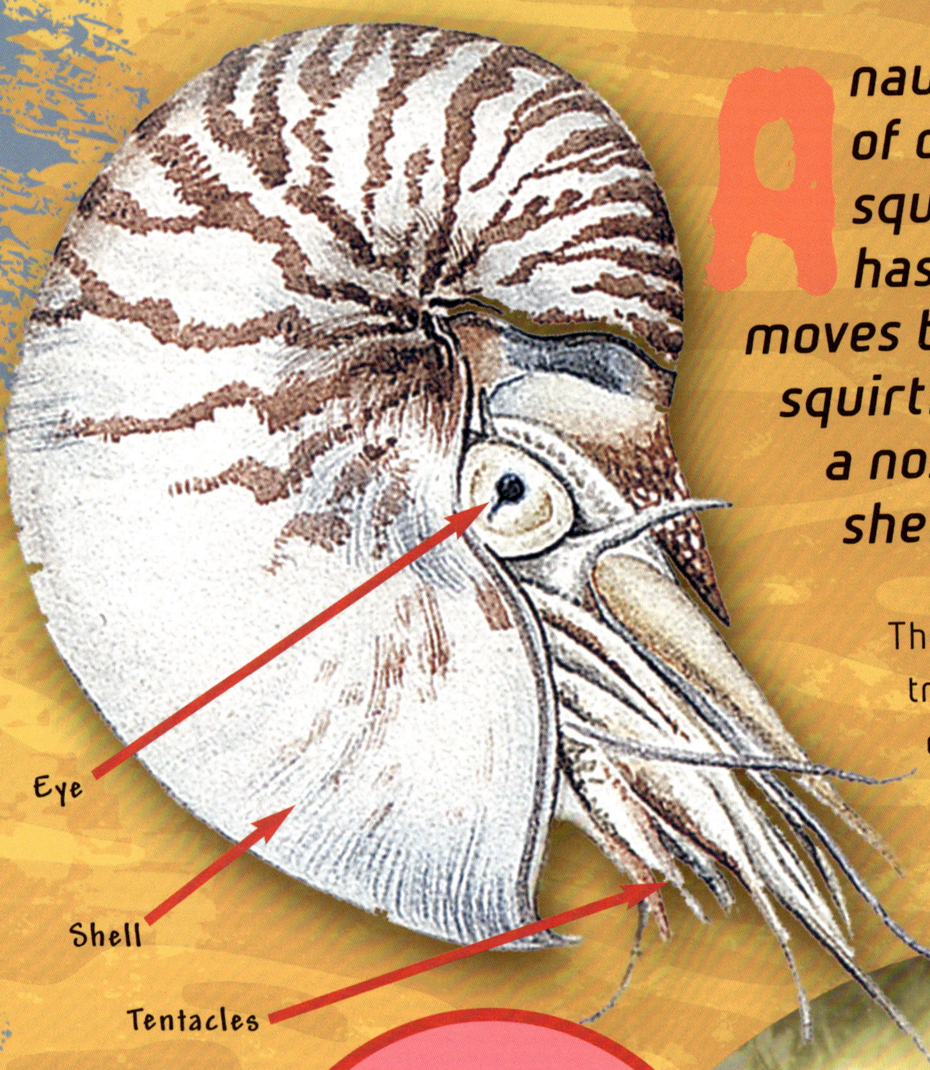

A nautilus is a relative of octopuses and squids, but it still has its shell. It moves by jet power, squirting water out of a nozzle so it swims shell first.

The nautilus is a hunter. It tracks small crabs and other crustaceans on the seafloor and grabs them with its many tentacles. Unlike its relatives, the nautilus does not have suckers on its tentacles. Scientists think that nautilus is a "living fossil." It is what the relatives of today's octopuses and squids looked like hundreds of millions of years ago.

Defenses

Unlike octopuses and squids, nautiluses do not have ink sacs to scare away attackers. However, they can pull their tentacles into their shell for safety.

UP CLOSE

A nautilus lives in just the largest chamber of its shell. As it grows, the nautilus builds walls inside the shell, sealing off the old chambers. The empty chambers are filled with gas and help the nautilus to float.

Common name:
Nautilus

Scientific name:
Nautilidae

Size: 10 in (25 cm) across

Key features: Fleshy body inside a coiled shell; 80 to 90 tentacles; simple eyes without a **lens**

Diet: Crustaceans

Gas Pipe

A special tube runs through the shell's chambers. It controls the amount of gas in the shell, so the nautilus floats or sinks.

SPINY SQUAT

If you see one squat lobster, you will probably see hundreds of them swarming over the seabed. They can give a nasty nip with their pincers. These creeping critters are the ocean's garbage collectors.

Spiny squat lobsters are omnivores, which means they eat anything. They clamber over the seabed clearing away the sludge of and bits of dead animals. When it is time to rest, they back into a hiding place to stay out of sight.

UP CLOSE

Squat lobsters are covered in spiky hairs. These are good at collecting food. Algae and other floating tidbits are trapped by the hairs and then swallowed.

LOBSTER

Common name: Spiny squat lobster
Scientific name: *Galathea strigosa*
Size: 20 in (50 cm)
Key features: Body covered in spines; six main legs, two small legs at the back; pincers longer than body
Diet: Fish, worms, dead animals, algae

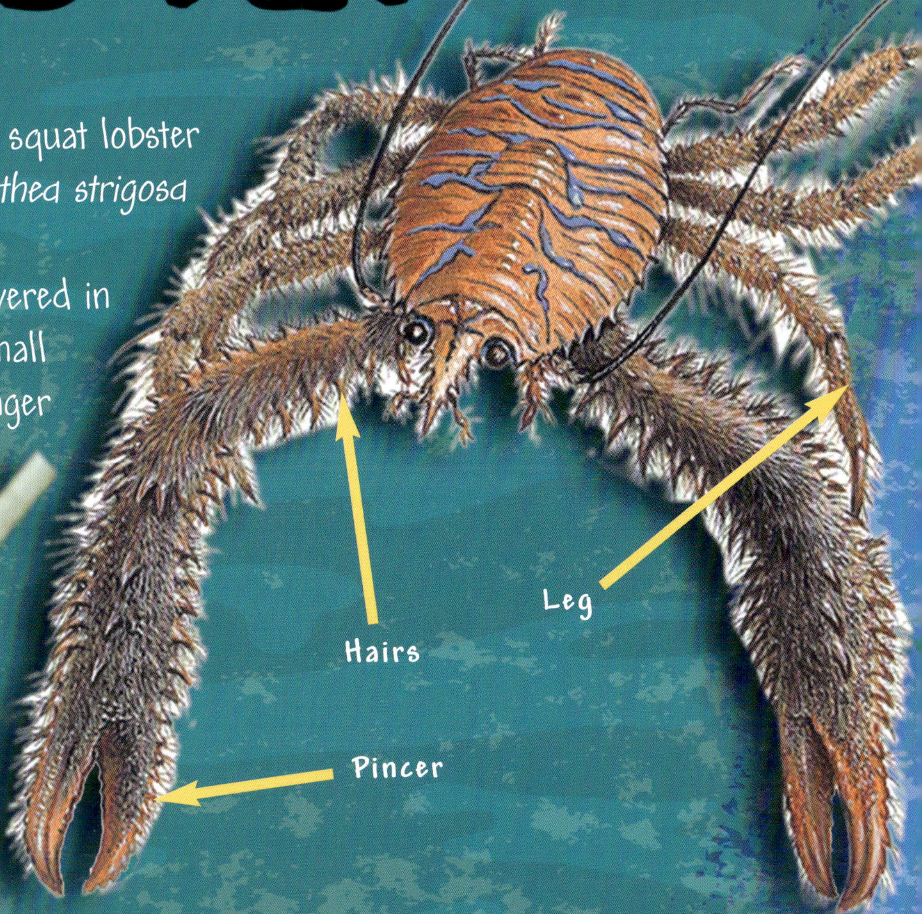

Big Nipper

The pincers, or chelipeds, of a squat lobster are three times longer than its body. The pincers are used to fight off attackers. Lobsters have to fight a lot—there is nowhere to hide when they are feeding in open water.

Swimming

Unlike most crabs or lobsters, squat lobsters are good swimmers, especially when they are young. They move through the water using a tail that is folded under the body the rest of the time.

GLOSSARY

algae Small, plantlike life-forms that float in water

barbels The fleshy whiskers around a fish's mouth; catfish are named for their long barbels like a cat's whiskers

camouflage A coloring or body shape that helps an animal to blend with—and hide in—its surroundings

cell A tiny building block of a living body; most bodies contain trillions of cells

dorsal fin The pointed fin on the back

fang A long, pointed tooth

flukes Flattened tail fins on a whale or dolphin that stick out sideways

lateral line A sensor that runs down the side of a fish and picks up movements in the water

lens A see-through body part that bends light inside the eye so it forms a clear picture of the outside world

lure To draw toward

mottled Blotchy coloring

nerves Special cells that carry messages around a living body

organ A part of a living thing that does a special job

plankton Animals and plants that cannot swim well and float around in ocean currents

polar To do with the cold North and South Poles

prey An animal that is hunted by another animal

saliva Spit, the liquid produced in the mouth to help with swallowing food

temperature A measure of how hot or cold something is

tentacle Long, flexible arm

tropical To do with the warm areas of Earth around the equator (an imaginary line running around the center of Earth)

venom A poisonous liquid that some animals produce. They inject the poison into their victims by biting it.

virus A tiny creature that can only be seen with a microscope and often causes diseases

FURTHER RESOURCES

Books about sea monsters

Batson, Peter. *Creatures of the Deep*. New York, NY: Tangerine Press, 2008.

Blaxland, Beth. *Octopuses, Squids, and Their Relatives: Cephalopods*. Philadelphia, PA: Chelsea House Publishers, 2003.

Jackson, Tom. *Monster Crocs*. New York, NY: Crabtree, 2008.

Jango-Cohen, Judith. *Real-life Sea Monsters* Minneapolis, MN: Millbrook Press, 2008.

Regan Barnhill, Kelly. *Monsters of the Deep*. Mankato, MN: Capstone Press, 2008.

Useful Web sites

Leichhardt's Sawfish
http://www.arkive.org/leichhardts-sawfish/pristis-microdon/facts-and-status.html

MarineBio: Blue-ringed Octopus
http://marinebio.org/species.asp?id=403

National Geographic: Saltwater Crocodile
http://animals.nationalgeographic.com/animals/reptiles/saltwater-crocodile/

Publisher's note to educators and parents: Our editors have carefully reviewed these Web sites to ensure that they are suitable for students. Many Web sites change frequently, however, and we cannot guarantee that a site's future contents will continue to meet our high standards of quality and educational value. Be advised that students should be closely supervised whenever they access the Internet.

INDEX